JAZO · DM 3.-

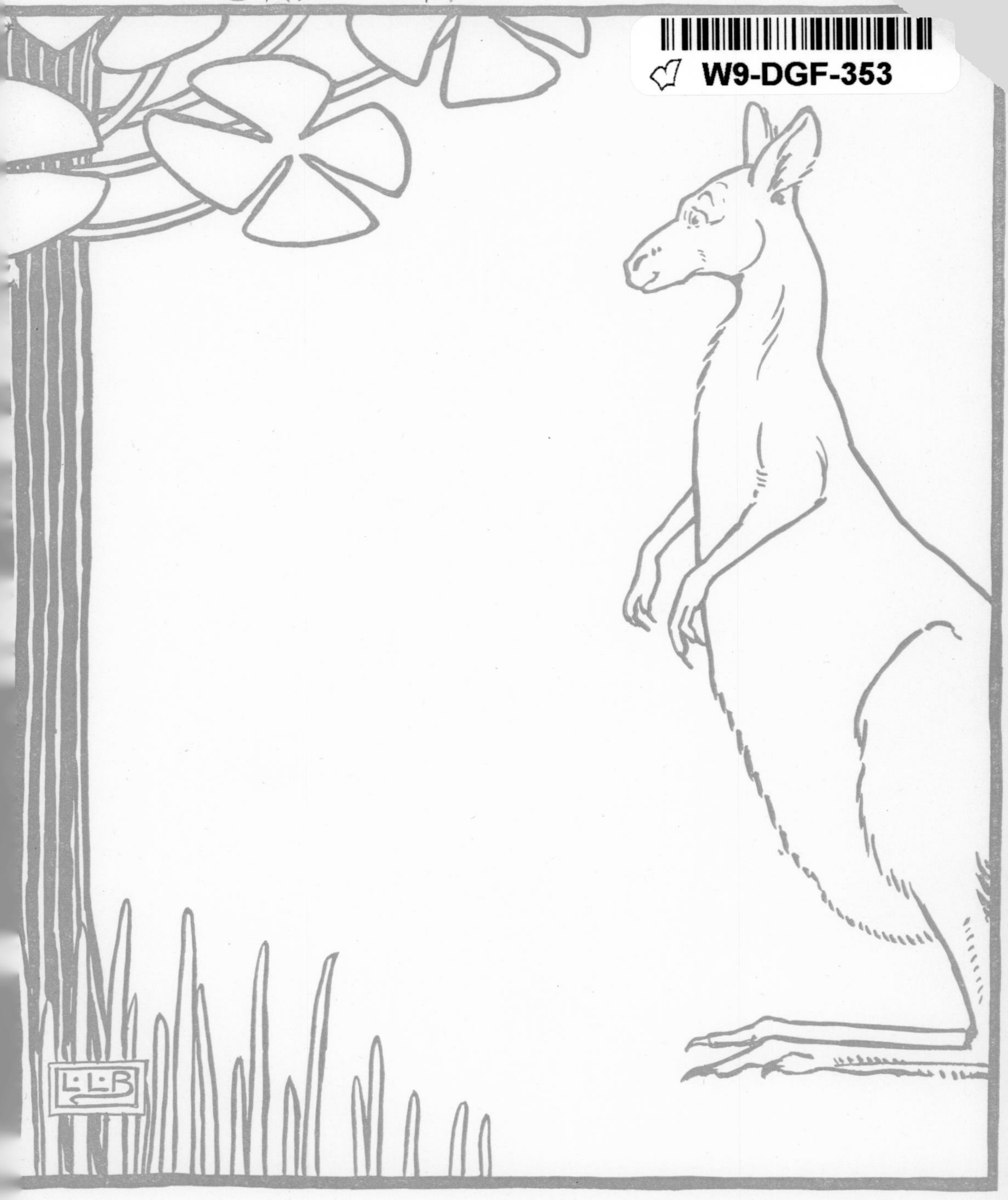

THE PELICAN CHORUS
AND
OTHER NONSENSE VERSES

FREDERICK WARNE & CO. LTD.
LONDON ENGLAND

ISBN 0 7232 0584 1

PRINTED IN GREAT BRITAIN
BY COMPTON PRINTING LTD., AYLESBURY

727.1273

THE PELICAN CHORUS

&

OTHER
NONSENSE VERSES BY
EDWARD LEAR
AUTHOR OF 'THE BOOK OF NONSENSE'

WITH DRAWINGS BY
L·LESLIE BROOKE

FREDERICK WARNE & CO LTD
LONDON   NEW YORK

PREFACE

After many years of publication of the famous Nonsense Songs by Edward Lear which were originally illustrated by the Author himself, it was felt by the publishers that Mr. Lear had, contrary to his usual custom, presented these songs illustrated in the slightest manner only. Mr. L. Leslie Brooke therefore endeavoured to create a further and wider interest in the verses by his own interpretation of them, with many line drawings and colour plates.

The unwonted pleasure the verses have given to thousands of readers will, it is felt, be fully maintained in this further edition with Mr. L. Leslie Brooke's illustrations.

Sir Edward Strachey said in his Introduction to "Nonsense Songs and Stories" under the heading of

WHAT IS NONSENSE?

"From the days when Aristotle investigated the philosophy of laughter, and Aristophanes gave laughter its fullest—I might say its maddest—expression on the stage at Athens, down to this week's issue of *Punch*, Nonsense has asserted and made good its claim to a place among the Arts. It has indeed pressed each of them in turn into its service. Nonsense has found the highest expression of itself in music, painting, sculpture, and every form of poetry and prose. The so-called Nonsense Club, which could count Hogarth and Cowper among its members, must have been worthy of the name, for so we have the 'March to Finchley' and 'John Gilpin' to testify; but as far as I know, Edward Lear first openly gave Nonsense its due place and honour when he called what he wrote pure and absolute Nonsense, and gave the affix of 'Nonsense' to every kind of subject; and while we may say, as Johnson did of Goldsmith, that there was hardly a subject which he did not handle, we may add with Johnson that there was none that he did not adorn by his handling. His pen and pencil vied with each other in pouring forth new kinds of Nonsense Songs, Nonsense Stories, Nonsense Alphabets and Nonsense Botany. The music to which he set the 'Pelican Chorus' is worthy of the words to which it is wedded; and those who remember the humorous melancholy with which the old man sat down at the piano to play and sing this song, will give his Nonsense Music a place too."

CONTENTS

The Pelican Chorus

THE PELICANS

King and Queen of the Peli - cans we, No other birds so grand we see!

None but we have feet like fins, With love - ly lea - the - ry throats and chins.

Coro—più sostenuto.

Ploff skin, Pluff - skin, Pe - li can Jee! We think no birds so hap - py as we!

Plump - skin, Ploff - skin, Pe - li - can Jill! We think so then, and we thought so still!

NOTE.—The air of this Song by Edward Lear; the arrangement for the piano by Professor Pomè, of San Remo, Italy.

THE PELICAN CHORUS

KING and Queen of the Pelicans we;
No other Birds so grand we see!
None but we have feet like fins!
With lovely leathery throats and chins!
    Ploffskin, Pluffskin, Pelican jee!
      We think no birds so happy as we!
    Plumpskin, Ploshkin, Pelican jill!
      We think so then, and we thought so still!

We live on the Nile. The Nile we love.
By night we sleep on the cliffs above.

The Pelican Chorus

By day we fish, and at eve we stand
On long bare islands of yellow sand.
And when the sun sinks slowly down
And the great rock walls grow dark and brown,
Where the purple river rolls fast and dim
And the ivory Ibis starlike skim,
Wing to wing we dance around,
Stamping our feet with a flumpy sound,
Opening our mouths as Pelicans ought,
And this is the song we nightly snort:
    Ploffskin, Pluffskin, Pelican jee,
      We think no Birds so happy as we!
    Plumpskin, Ploshkin, Pelican jill,
      We think so then, and we thought so still!

Last year came out our Daughter, Dell;
And all the Birds received her well.
To do her honour, a feast we made
For every bird that can swim or wade.
Herons and Gulls, and Cormorants black,
Cranes, and Flamingoes with scarlet back,
Plovers and Storks, and Geese in clouds,
Swans and Dilberry Ducks in crowds.
Thousands of Birds in wondrous flight!
They ate and drank and danced all night,
And echoing back from the rocks you heard
Multitude-echoes from Bird and Bird—

The Pelican Chorus

Ploffskin, Pluffskin, Pelican jee,
We think no Birds so happy as we!
Plumpskin, Ploshkin, Pelican jill,
We think so then, and we thought so still!

Yes, they came; and among the rest,
The King of the Cranes all grandly dressed

The Pelican Chorus

Such a lovely tail! Its feathers float
Between the ends of his blue dress-coat;
With pea-green trousers all so neat,
And a delicate frill to hide his feet,
(For though no one speaks of it, every one knows
He has got no webs between his toes!)

As soon as he saw our Daughter Dell,
In violent love that Crane King fell,
On seeing her waddling form so fair,
With a wreath of shrimps in her short white hair,
And before the end of the next long day,
Our Dell had given her heart away;
For the King of the Cranes had won that heart,
With a Crocodile's egg and a large fish-tart.
She vowed to marry the King of the Cranes,
Leaving the Nile for stranger plains;
And away they flew in a gathering crowd
Of endless birds in a lengthening cloud.
    Ploffskin, Pluffskin, Pelican jee,
      We think no Birds so happy as we!
    Plumpskin, Ploshkin, Pelican jill,
      We think so then, and we thought so still!

And far away in the twilight sky,
We heard them singing a lessening cry,

Farther and farther till out of sight,
And we stood alone in the silent night!
Often since, in the nights of June,
We sit on the sand and watch the moon;
She has gone to the great Gromboolian plain
And we probably never shall meet again!

The Pelican Chorus

Oft, in the long still nights of June,
We sit on the rocks and watch the moon;
——She dwells by the streams of the Chankly Bore,
And we probably never shall see her more.
    Ploffskin, Pluffskin, Pelican jee,
    We think no Birds so happy as we!
    Plumpskin, Ploshkin, Pelican jill,
    We think so then, and we thought so still!

MR. AND MRS. SPIKKY SPARROW

I

ON a little piece of wood,
Mr. Spikky Sparrow stood;
Mrs. Sparrow sate close by,
A-making of an insect pie,
For her little children five,
In the nest and all alive,
Singing with a cheerful smile
To amuse them all the while,
    Twikky wikky wikky we,
    Wikky bikky twikky tee,
    Spikky bikky bee!

II

Mrs. Spikky Sparrow said,
"Spikky, Darling! in my head
Many thoughts of trouble come,
Like to flies upon a plum!

Mr. and Mrs. Spikky Sparrow

All last night, among the trees,
I heard you cough, I heard you sneeze;
And, thought I, it's come to that
Because he does not wear a hat!
    Chippy wippy sikky tee!
    Bikky wikky tikky mee!
      Spikky chippy we!

III

"Not that you are growing old,
But the nights are growing cold.
No one stays out all night long
Without a hat: I'm sure it's wrong!"
Mr. Spikky said, "How kind,
Dear! you are, to speak your mind!
All your life I wish you luck!
You are! you are! a lovely duck!
    Witchy witchy witchy we!
    Twitchy witchy witchy bee!
      Tikky tikky tee!

IV

"I was also sad, and thinking,
When one day I saw you winking.
And I heard you sniffle-snuffle,
And I saw your feathers ruffle;

Mr. and Mrs. Spikky Sparrow

To myself I sadly said,
She's neuralgia in her head!
That dear head has nothing on it!
Ought she not to wear a bonnet?
    Witchy kitchy kitchy wee!
    Spikky wikky mikky bee!
        Chippy wippy chee!

Mr. and Mrs. Spikky Sparrow

V

"Let us both fly up to town!
There I'll buy you such a gown!
Which, completely in the fashion,
You shall tie a sky-blue sash on.
And a pair of slippers neat,
To fit your darling little feet,
So that you will look and feel
Quite galloobious and genteel!
    Jikky wikky bikky see!
    Chicky bikky wikky bee!
    Twicky witchy wee!"

VI

So they both to London went,
Alighting on the Monument,
Whence they flew down swiftly—pop,
Into Moses' wholesale shop;
There they bought a hat and bonnet,
And a gown with spots upon it,
A satin sash of Cloxam blue,
And a pair of slippers too.
    Zikky wikky mikky bee!
    Witchy witchy mitchy kee!
    Sikky tikky wee!

VII

Then when so completely drest,
Back they flew and reached their nest.
Their children cried, "O Ma and Pa!
How truly beautiful you are!"
Said they, "We trust that cold or pain
We shall never feel again!
While perched on tree, or house, or steeple,
We now shall look like other people.
    Witchy witchy witchy wee!
    Twikky mikky bikky bee!
    Zikky sikky tee!"

The Table and The Chair.

THE TABLE AND THE CHAIR

I

SAID the Table to the Chair,
"You can hardly be aware
How I suffer from the heat,
And from chilblains on my feet!
If we took a little walk,
We might have a little talk!
Pray let us take the air!"
Said the Table to the Chair.

II

Said the Chair unto the Table,
"Now you *know* we are not able!
How foolishly you talk,
When you know we *cannot* walk!"
Said the Table with a sigh,
"It can do no harm to try;
I've as many legs as you,
Why can't we walk on two?"

III

So they both went slowly down,
And walked about the town
With a cheerful bumpy sound,
As they toddled round and round.
And everybody cried,
As they hastened to their side,
"See! the Table and the Chair
Have come out to take the air!"

IV

But in going down an alley,
To a castle in the valley,
They completely lost their way,
And wandered all the day,
Till, to see them safely back,
They paid a Ducky-quack,

And a Beetle, and a Mouse,
Who took them to their house.

V

Then they whispered to each other,
"O delightful little brother!
What a lovely walk we've taken!
Let us dine on Beans and Bacon!"
So the Ducky and the leetle
Browny-Mousy and the Beetle
Dined, and danced upon their heads
Till they toddled to their beds.

THE DADDY LONG-LEGS AND THE FLY

I

ONCE Mr. Daddy Long-legs,
  Dressed in brown and gray,
Walked about upon the sands
  Upon a summer's day;
And there among the pebbles,
  When the wind was rather cold,
He met with Mr. Floppy Fly,
  All dressed in blue and gold.
And as it was too soon to dine,
They drank some Periwinkle-wine,
And played an hour or two, or more,
At battlecock and shuttledore.

II

Said Mr. Daddy Long-legs
  To Mr. Floppy Fly,
"Why do you never come to court?
  I wish you'd tell me why.
All gold and shine, in dress so fine,
  You'd quite delight the court.
Why do you never go at all?
  I really think you *ought*!
And if you went, you'd see such sights!
Such rugs! and jugs! and candle-lights!
And more than all, the King and Queen,
One in red, and one in green!"

III

"O Mr. Daddy Long-legs,"
  Said Mr. Floppy Fly,
"It's true I never go to court,
  And I will tell you why.
If I had six long legs like yours,
  At once I'd go to court!
But oh! I can't, because *my* legs
  Are so extremely short.
And I'm afraid the King and Queen
(One in red, and one in green)
Would say aloud, 'You are not fit,
You Fly, to come to court a bit!' "

IV

"O Mr. Daddy Long-legs,"
    Said Mr. Floppy Fly,
"I wish you'd sing one little song!
    One mumbian melody!
You used to sing so awful well
    In former days gone by,
But now you never sing at all;
    I wish you'd tell me why:
For if you would, the silvery sound
Would please the shrimps and cockles round,
And all crabs would gladly come
To hear you sing, 'Ah, Hum di Hum!'"

V

Said Mr. Daddy Long-legs,
    "I can never sing again!
And if you wish, I'll tell you why,
    Although it gives me pain.
For years I could not hum a bit,
    Or sing the smallest song;
And this the dreadful reason is,
    My legs are grown too long!
My six long legs, all here and there,
Oppress my bosom with despair;
And if I stand, or lie, or sit,
I cannot sing one single bit!"

VI

So Mr. Daddy Long-legs
   And Mr. Floppy Fly
Sat down in silence by the sea,
   And gazed upon the sky.

They said, "This is a dreadful thing!
   The world has all gone wrong,
Since one has legs too short by half,
   The other much too long!
One never more can go to court,
Because his legs have grown too short;
The other cannot sing a song,
Because his legs have grown too long!"

VII

Then Mr. Daddy Long-legs
　And Mr. Floppy Fly
Rushed downward to the foaming sea
　With one sponge-taneous cry;

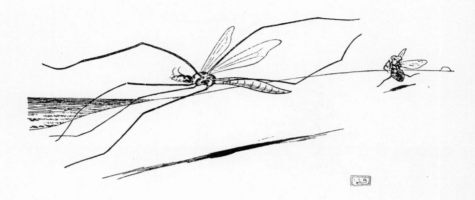

And there they found a little boat,
　Whose sails were pink and gray;
And off they sailed among the waves,
　Far, and far away.
They sailed across the silent main,
And reached the great Gromboolian plain;
And there they play for evermore
At battlecock and shuttledore

MR. AND MRS. DISCOBBOLOS

I

MR. AND MRS. DISCOBBOLOS
Climbed to the top of a wall,
And they sat to watch the sunset sky,
And to hear the Nupiter Piffkin cry
And the Biscuit Buffalo call.
They took up a roll and some Camomile tea,
And both were as happy as happy could be—
Till Mrs. Discobbolos said,
"Oh! W! X! Y! Z!
It has just come into my head—
Suppose we should happen to fall!!!!!
Darling Mr. Discobbolos!

Mr. and Mrs. Discobbolos

II

"Suppose we should fall down flumpetty
  Just like two pieces of stone!
On to the thorns—or into the moat!
What would become of your new green coat?
  And might you not break a bone?
It never occurred to me before—
That perhaps we shall never go down any more!"
  And Mrs. Discobbolos said,
  "Oh! W! X! Y! Z!
  What put it into your head
To climb up this wall?—my own

Darling Mr. Discobbolos?"

III

Mr. Discobbolos answered,
 "At first it gave me pain,
 And I felt my ears turn perfectly pink
 When your exclamation made me think
  We might never get down again!
But now I believe it is wiser far
To remain for ever just where we are."
 And Mr. Discobbolos said,
 "Oh! W! X! Y! Z!
 It has just come into my head—
——We shall never go down again—
    Dearest Mrs. Discobbolos!"

IV

So, Mr. and Mrs. Discobbolos
 Stood up, and began to sing,
 "Far away from hurry and strife
 Here we will pass the rest of life,
  Ding a dong, ding dong, ding!
We want no knives nor forks nor chairs,
No tables nor carpets nor household cares,

Mr. and Mrs. Discobbolos

From worry of life we've fled—
Oh! W! X! Y! Z!
There is no more trouble ahead
Sorrow or any such thing—
    For Mr. and Mrs. Discobbolos!"

The Two Old Bachelors

THE TWO OLD BACHELORS

TWO old Bachelors were living in one house;
One caught a Muffin, the other caught a Mouse.
Said he who caught the Muffin to him who caught the
Mouse,

"This happens just in time! For we've nothing in the
     house,
Save a tiny slice of lemon and a teaspoonful of honey.
And what to do for dinner—since we haven't any
     money?
And what can we expect if we haven't any dinner,
But to lose our teeth and eyelashes and keep on
     growing thinner?"

Said he who caught the Mouse to him who caught the
     Muffin,
"We might cook this little Mouse, if we only had some
     Stuffin'!
If we had but Sage and Onion we could do extremely
     well,
But how to get that Stuffin' it is difficult to tell!"

Those two old Bachelors ran quickly to the town
And asked for Sage and Onion as they wandered up
     and down;
They borrowed two large Onions, but no Sage was to
     be found
In the Shops, or in the Market, or in all the Gardens
     round.

But some one said, "A hill there is, a little to the north,
And to its purpledicular top a narrow way leads forth;
And there among the rugged rocks abides an ancient
    Sage,
An earnest Man, who reads all day a most perplexing
    page.
Climb up, and seize him by the toes!—all studious as
    he sits,
And pull him down, and chop him into endless little
    bits!
Then mix him with your Onion (cut up likewise into
    Scraps),
When your Stuffin' will be ready—and very good:
    perhaps."

Those two old Bachelors without loss of time
The nearly purpledicular crags at once began to climb;
And at the top, among the rocks, all seated in a
    nook,
They saw that Sage a-reading of a most enormous
    book.
"You earnest Sage!" aloud they cried, "your book you've
    read enough in!—
We wish to chop you into bits to mix you into
    Stuffin'!"

But that old Sage looked calmly up, and with his awful
    book,

At those two Bachelors' bald heads a certain aim he
    took;

And over crag and precipice they rolled promiscuous
    down,

At once they rolled, and never stopped in lane or field
    or town,

And when they reached their house, they found (besides
    their want of Stuffin'),

The Mouse had fled; and, previously, had eaten up the
    Muffin.

They left their home in silence by the once convivial
    door,
And from that hour those Bachelors were never heard
    of more.

THE POBBLE WHO HAS NO TOES

I

THE Pobble who has no toes
   Had once as many as we;
When they said, "Some day you may lose them all";
   He replied, "Fish fiddle de-dee!"
And his Aunt Jobiska made him drink
Lavender water tinged with pink,
For she said, "The World in general knows
There's nothing so good for a Pobble's toes!"

II

The Pobble who has no toes
   Swam across the Bristol Channel;

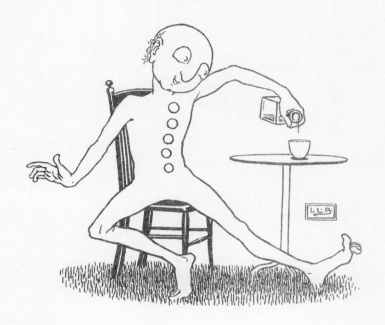

But before he set out he wrapped his nose
    In a piece of scarlet flannel.
For his Aunt Jobiska said, "No harm
Can come to his toes if his nose is warm;
And it's perfectly known that a Pobble's toes
Are safe—provided he minds his nose."

III

The Pobble swam fast and well,
    And when boats or ships came near him

He tinkledy-binkledy-winkled a bell,
  So that all the world could hear him.
And all the Sailors and Admirals cried,

When they saw him nearing the further side,
"He has gone to fish, for his Aunt Jobiska's
Runcible Cat with crimson whiskers!"

IV

But before he touched the shore,
   The shore of the Bristol Channel,
A sea-green Porpoise carried away
   His wrapper of scarlet flannel.
And when he came to observe his feet,
Formerly garnished with toes so neat,
His face at once became forlorn
On perceiving that all his toes were gone!

V

And nobody ever knew
   From that dark day to the present,
Whoso had taken the Pobble's toes,
   In a manner so far from pleasant,
Whether the shrimps or crawfish gray,
Or crafty Mermaids stole them away—
Nobody knew; and nobody knows
How the Pobble was robbed of his twice five toes!

VI

The Pobble who has no toes
   Was placed in a friendly Bark,

And they rowed him back, and carried him up
   To his Aunt Jobiska's Park.
And she made him a feast at his earnest wish
Of eggs and buttercups fried with fish;
And she said, "It's a fact the whole world knows,
That Pobbles are happier without their toes."

The Quangle Wangle's Hat.

THE QUANGLE WANGLE'S HAT

I

ON the top of the Crumpetty Tree
   The Quangle Wangle sat,
But his face you could not see,
   On account of his Beaver Hat.
For his Hat was a hundred and two feet wide,
With ribbons and bibbons on every side,
And bells, and buttons, and loops, and lace,
So that nobody ever could see the face
     Of the Quangle Wangle Quee.

II

The Quangle Wangle said
   To himself on the Crumpetty Tree,
"Jam; and jelly; and bread;
   Are the best of food for me!

But the longer I live on this Crumpetty Tree,
The plainer than ever it seems to me
That very few people come this way,
And that life on the whole is far from gay!"
    Said the Quangle Wangle Quee.

III

But there came to the Crumpetty Tree,
    Mr. and Mrs. Canary;
And they said, "Did ever you see
    Any spot so charmingly airy?
May we build a nest on your lovely Hat?
Mr. Quangle Wangle, grant us that!
O please let us come and build a nest
Of whatever material suits you best,
        Mr. Quangle Wangle Quee!"

IV

And besides, to the Crumpetty Tree
    Came the Stork, the Duck, and the Owl;
The Snail and the Bumble-Bee,
    The Frog and the Fimble Fowl;
(The Fimble Fowl, with a Corkscrew leg);
And all of them said, "We humbly beg,
We may build our homes on your lovely Hat,
Mr. Quangle Wangle, grant us that!
        Mr. Quangle Wangle Quee!"

V

And the Golden Grouse came there,
    And the Pobble who has no toes,
And the small Olympian bear,
    And the Dong with a luminous nose.
And the Blue Baboon, who played the flute,
And the Orient Calf from the Land of Tute,

And the Attery Squash, and the Bisky Bat,
All came and built on the lovely Hat
   Of the Quangle Wangle Quee.

VI

And the Quangle Wangle said
   To himself on the Crumpetty Tree,
"When all these creatures move
   What a wonderful noise there'll be!"
And at night by the light of the Mulberry moon
They danced to the Flute of the Blue Baboon,
On the broad green leaves of the Crumpetty Tree,
And all were as happy as happy could be,
   With the Quangle Wangle Quee.

THE NUTCRACKERS AND THE SUGAR-TONGS

I

THE Nutcrackers sate by a plate on the table,
   The Sugar-tongs sate by a plate at his side;
And the Nutcrackers said, "Don't you wish we were
      able
    Along the blue hills and green meadows to ride?
Must we drag on this stupid existence for ever,
   So idle and weary, so full of remorse,
While every one else takes his pleasure, and never
   Seems happy unless he is riding a horse?

II

"Don't you think we could ride without being instructed?
   Without any saddle, or bridle, or spur?
Our legs are so long, and so aptly constructed,
   I'm sure that an accident could not occur.

Let us all of a sudden hop down from the table,
   And hustle downstairs, and each jump on a horse!
Shall we try? Shall we go? Do you think we are able?"
   The Sugar-tongs answered distinctly, "Of course!"

III

So down the long staircase they hopped in a minute,
   The Sugar-tongs snapped, and the Crackers said,
      "Crack!"
The stable was open, the horses were in it;
   Each took out a pony, and jumped on his back.
The Cat in a fright scrambled out of the doorway,
   The Mice tumbled out of a bundle of hay,
The brown and white Rats, and the black ones from
      Norway,
   Screamed out, "They are taking the horses away!"

IV

The whole of the household was filled with amazement,
   The Cups and the Saucers danced madly about,
The Plates and the Dishes looked out of the casement,
   The Saltcellar stood on his head with a shout,
The Spoons with a clatter looked out of the lattice,
   The Mustard-pot climbed up the Gooseberry Pies,
The Soup-ladle peeped through a heap of Veal Patties,
   And squeaked with a ladle-like scream of surprise.

V

The Frying-pan said, "It's an awful delusion!"

The Tea-kettle hissed
and grew black in
the face;
And they all rushed
downstairs in the
wildest confusion,
To see the great Nut-
cracker-Sugar-tong
race.
And out of the stable,
with screamings
and laughter,
(Their ponies were
cream-coloured,
speckled with
brown),
The Nutcrackers first,
and the Sugar-tongs
after,
Rode all round the yard, and then all round the
town.

VI

They rode through the street, and they rode by the
    station,
  They galloped away to the beautiful shore;
In silence they rode, and "made no observation",
  Save this: "We will never go back any more!"
And still you might hear, till they rode out of hearing,
  The Sugar-tongs snap, and the Crackers say "Crack!"
Till far in the distance, their forms disappearing,
  They faded away.—And they never came back!